with you

Coping with the Loss of a Loved One

Susan V. Bertram

BRAVEN ART

Los Gatos, California

WITH YOU:
COPING WITH THE LOSS OF A LOVED ONE

www.BravenArt.com

ISBN-13: 978-0-615-89626-7
ISBN-10: 0-615-89626-X

Illustrations by Joe Di Guiseppi and Susan V. Bertram
Prepared for publication by Kelly Tunstall

for Grandma Virginia

I have learned that we are
all connected and

I will tell you how.

When my mother was a baby,
my grandmother took care of her.

She bathed her, fed her, played with her
and loved her the best way she knew how.

She loved her.

When I was a baby, Grandma
sometimes took care of me, too.

She bathed me, fed me,
played with me and loved me
the best way she knew how.

She loved me.

As I got bigger, the body Grandma's spirit
lived in became old and tired.

So I helped bathe her, feed her, play with her
and love her the best way I knew how.

I loved her and she loved me.

I know that Grandma's body is just like a
little house that her spirit lives in for a while.

When her spirit becomes too big for the house,
her spirit will rise up and she will become one with
everything around me, including myself.

She will be part of the
rain, sun, wind, and trees.

I know that when it rains,
it will be her tapping me on the head saying,

"Hello there! I love you."

I will say, "I love you, too, Grandma."

When I feel the hot sun on my skin,
I will know it is her hugging me and saying,

"I love you."

It will feel very good and I will say,
"Thank you. I love you, too"

and I will give her a hug.

When I hear the wind swirling around me,
I will know she is playing with me.
I will say, "Run with me, Grandma!
You can't catch me!" We will run together.

We will laugh and I will hear her say, "I love you"
and I will say, "I love you, too, Grandma!
Thank you for coming to visit me."

When I climb high up into a tree
and find a comfy place to sit,

I will know that I am sitting in her
comfy lap and she is holding me.

I will say, "Grandma, tell me a story" and

I will hear her stories inside of me.

When I eat the vegetables from our garden,
I will know she is feeding me.

She loves to watch me grow healthy and strong.

She is proud of me.

So I say, "Thank you, Grandma.
I know that you are a part of me."

This will make me very happy.
I will say, "Thank you."

As I grow older, I know more people I love will become too big for their houses.

Their little houses will no longer serve them.
Some will be young and some will be old.
But it is all the same. We are all one.

I will continue to take care of them and they will continue to take care of me.

That is the way it should be.

When I see a stranger, I smile and say hello
because I know a little bit of my grandmother
is within them, and a little bit of me, too.

The same bright sun shines upon them.
The same wind sings in their ears and caresses them.

The same rain taps them on the head.
The same earth helps them grow.

I smile and say hello to all of them.

One day, I will grow too big for my house.
I will rise up and shine. This will be a magical day.

I will help the sun grow hotter. As the wind, I will
sing quietly in your ear and play with you.

I will be the rain that taps you on the head.

My grandmother and I will help you grow too big for your
little house. We will one day say....

"Rise up!

Come play with us!"

Susan V. Bertram

Thank you to those I have loved and cared for;
and who have loved and cared for me.

May the wonders of this beautiful world continue to inspire
each of us to love and care for each other.

A special thanks to my brave and wonderful husband, Dan,
and to my four amazing children: Nick, Brandon, Isabella, and Aidan.